My Family
Mi familia

My Dad
Mi papá

Emily Sebastian

PowerKiDS press & Editorial Buenas Letras™

New York

For my dad

Published in 2011 by The Rosen Publishing Group, Inc.
29 East 21st Street, New York, NY 10010

Copyright © 2011 by The Rosen Publishing Group, Inc.

All rights reserved. No part of this book may be reproduced in any form without permission in writing from the publisher, except by a reviewer.

First Edition

Editor: Amelie von Zumbusch
Book Design: Ashley Burrell

Photo Researcher: Jessica Gerweck
Spanish Translation: Eduardo Alamán

Photo Credits: Cover Mel Yates/Getty Images; pp. 5, 7 (dad, mom) 14–15, 20–21, 23 Shutterstock.com; p. 7 (brother) © www.iStockphoto.com/Ekaterina Monakhova; p. 7 (sister) © www.iStockphoto.com/quavondo; p. 8 © www.iStockphoto.com/Steve Cole; p. 11 Chris Clinton/Getty Images; pp. 12–13 © www.iStockphoto.com/Lisa F. Young; p. 19 Jupiterimages/Getty Images; p. 16 Andersen Ross/Getty Images.

Library of Congress Cataloging-in-Publication Data

Sebastian, Emily.
  My dad = Mi papá / Emily Sebastian. — 1st ed.
    p. cm. — (My family = mi familia)
  Includes index.
  ISBN 978-1-4488-0981-3 (library binding)
  1. Fathers—Juvenile literature. 2. Father and child—Juvenile literature. I. Title. II. Title: Mi papá.
  HQ756.S433 2011b
  306.874′2—dc22

Manufactured in the United States of America

CPSIA Compliance Information: Batch #WS10PK: For Further Information contact Rosen Publishing, New York, New York at 1-800-237-9932

Web Sites: Due to the changing nature of Internet links, PowerKids Press and Editorial Buenas Letras have developed an online list of Web sites related to the subject of this book. This site is updated regularly. Please use this link to access the list: www.powerkidslinks.com/family/dad/

Contents / Contenido

Dads 4
What Do Dads Do? 9
Every Family Is Different 18
Words to Know 24
Index 24

Los papás 4
¿Qué hace papá? 9
Cada familia es distinta 18
Palabras que debes saber 24
Índice 24

Sara is playing with her dad. Latin American dads spend lots of time with their kids.

Sara juega con su papá. Los papás latinoamericanos pasan mucho tiempo con sus hijos.

A family tree shows how family members are **related**. Can you find the dad on this tree?

Un árbol genealógico nos muestra cómo **emparentan** los miembros de una familia. ¿Puedes encontrar al papá?

Family Tree / Árbol Genealógico

Dad / Papá

Mom / Mamá

Brother / Hermano

Sister / Hermana

Diego's dad is a doctor. Dads can have all sorts of jobs.

El papá de Diego es doctor. Los papás tienen toda clase de trabajos distintos.

Dads also do work around the house. This dad is ironing.

Los papás también ayudan en casa. Este papá está planchando.

11

Dads can teach you things. Alex's dad is teaching her to play the guitar.

Tu papá te puede enseñar cosas. El papá de Alex le enseña a tocar la guitarra.

If you need help, ask your dad! Daniel's dad helps him with his homework.

Tú puedes pedirle ayuda a tu papá. Aquí el papá de Daniel le ayuda con la tarea.

Kids often **celebrate** holidays with their dads. Spending holidays with family is an important part of Latin American culture.

Con frecuencia los chicos **celebran** las fiestas con sus papás. Pasar tiempo en familia es una parte muy importante de la cultura latinoamericana.

Some kids live with their dads. Others visit their dads on weekends.

Algunos chicos viven con su papá. Otros visitan a su papá los fines de semana.

Many kids have a stepdad. Sofia likes to eat breakfast with her stepdad.

Muchos chicos tienen un padrastro. Sofía disfruta desayunando con su padrastro.

Every dad is a little different. However, all dads love their kids.

Cada papá es distinto. ¡Sin embargo, todos los papás quieren mucho a sus hijos!

Words to Know / Palabras que debes saber

celebrate (SEH-leh-brayt) To honor an important moment by doing special things.
related (rih-LAYT-ed) Part of the same family.

celebración (la) Honrar un momento importante haciendo una actividad especial.
emparentado Ser parte de una familia.

Index | índice

F
family tree, 6

G
guitar, 12

K
kids, 4, 17–18, 20, 22

S
stepdad, 20

A
árbol genealógico, 6

C
chicos, 17–18, 20, 22

G
guitarra, 12

P
padrastro, 20